001–020. Architectural and sculptural painted ornament

021–038. Painted tomb ceilings and friezes

039–074. Floral ornament and frets from terra-cottas and vases

075–115. Ornament, chiefly architectural

116–137. Mosaics and murals from Pompeii and Herculaneum

138–157. Fragments of allover designs

158–168. Motifs from textiles of the 17th and 18th centuries

169–188. Motifs from textiles and wallpapers

189–220. Florals and scrollwork from textiles, manuscripts, and metalwork

221–234. Enamels, cloisonné, niello, and chased steel from Kashmir and the north

235–251. Border elements from 16th-century paintings

252–262. Carpet design and allover geometric designs from manuscripts

263–278. Motifs from enameled and glazed ceramic wall cladding

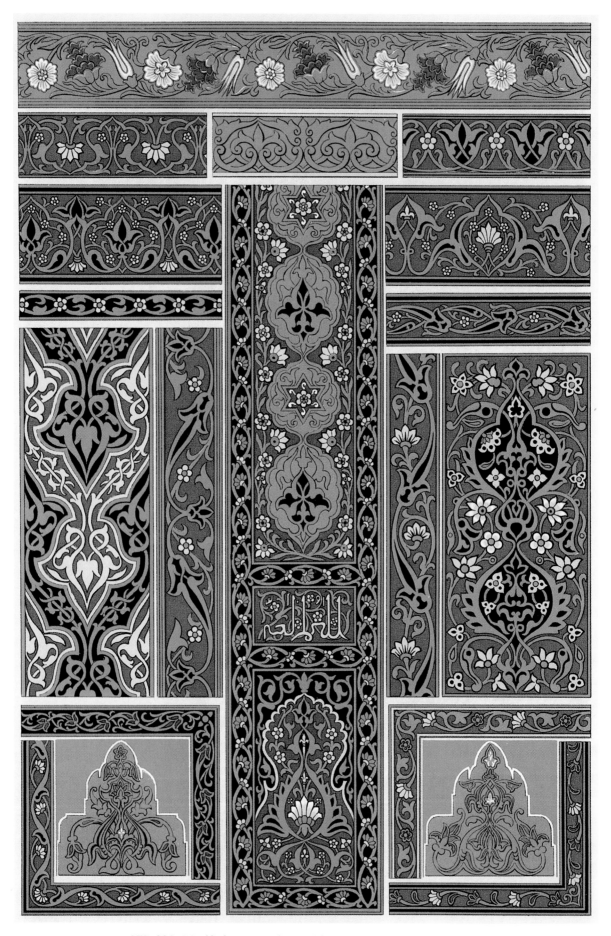

279–293. Motifs from exterior and interior faience wall cladding

294–303. Motifs from wall tiles, inlaid wood, and painted and enameled terra-cottas

304–326. Motifs from an illuminated Gospel manuscript, 16th century

327–347. Ornaments from an illuminated manuscript

348–361. Designs with lettering from an illuminated Koran, 14th or 15th century

362–380. Tile designs from the Alhambra and from the Seville Alcázar

381–405. Designs from architecture and manuscripts, Greece and Italy

406–425. Designs from mosaics (Sicily), frescoes (Asia Minor), and enamels

426–441. Mosaics from Palermo and Salerno

442–462. Mosaic patterns from Italian churches

463–493. Designs from ivory and wood inlays, France and Italy, 14th and 15th centuries

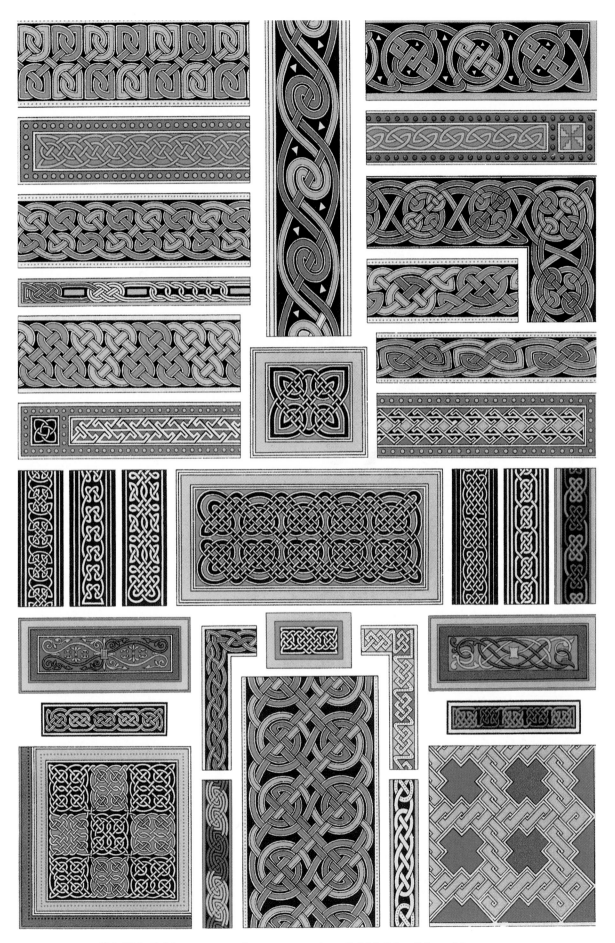

494–526. Celtic ornament from manuscripts, British Isles, 7th to 9th century

527–548. Designs from textiles depicted in 16th-century manuscript illuminations

549–555. Flowers and jewels from 15th-century manuscripts

556–565. Frames and ornaments from illuminated manuscripts, Western Europe

566–578. Mosaic and painted ornament, France, late Roman to Romanesque periods

579–590. Bas-reliefs, ironwork, and painting, France, 11th to 14th century

591–619. Stained glass from French and English cathedrals, 12th to 14th century

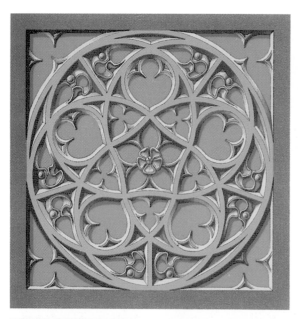

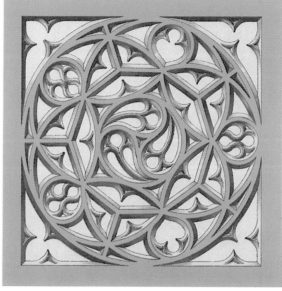

620–625. Painted and gilt woodwork, 15th century

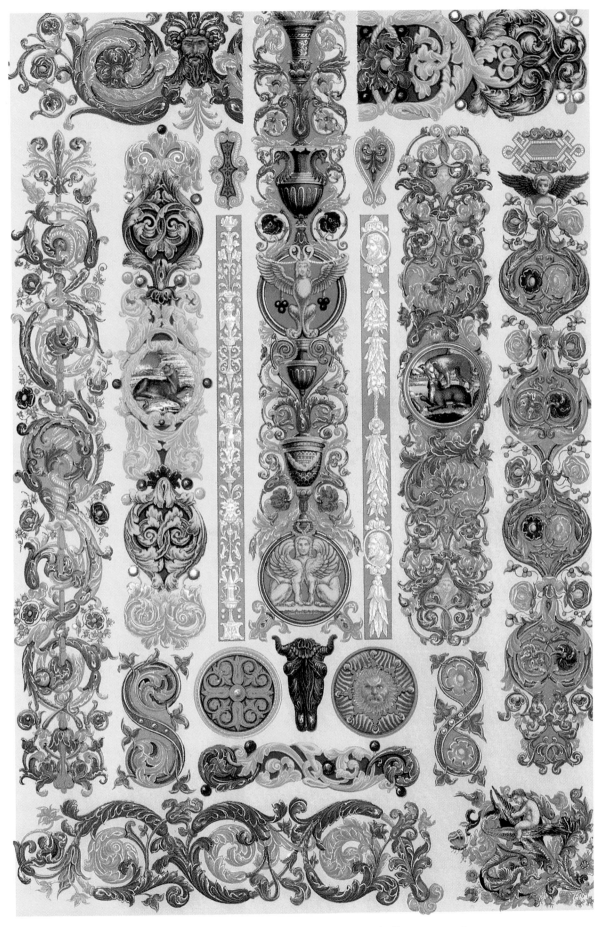

626–644. Ornaments from a late 15th-century Italian manuscript

645–664. Designs from engraved ivories, including furniture inlays

665–689. From Italian frescoes and manuscripts, 15th and 16th centuries

690–694. Borders from a Florentine manuscript by Attavante (1452 to ca. 1520)

695–710. Margin decorations from manuscripts, 15th and 16th centuries

711–729. Ornaments from Italian manuscripts, 16th and 17th centuries

730–748. From stained glass, tapestries, and sculpture, France, 16th century

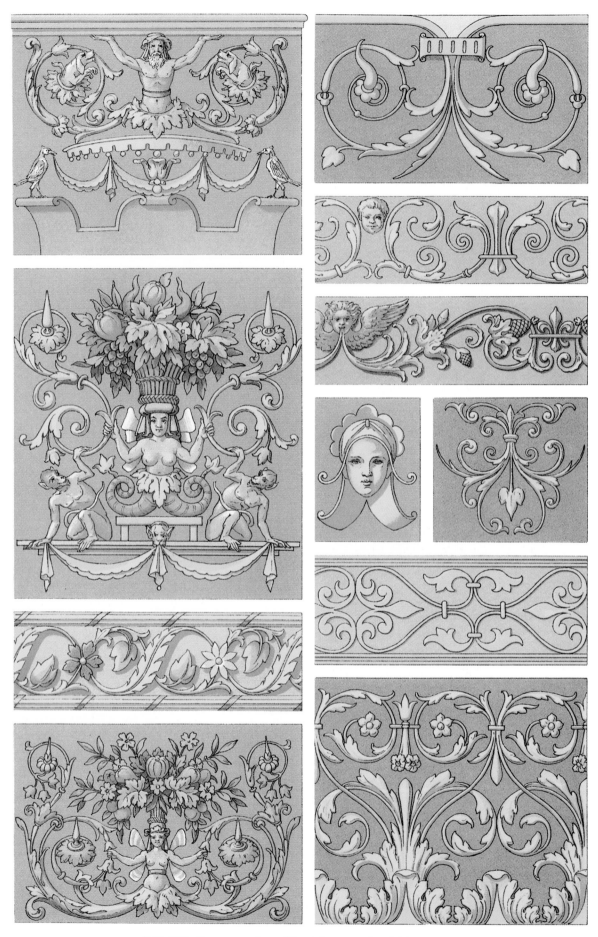

749–759. Ornament from Flemish tapestries, 16th century

760–779. Lace motifs from a volume published in Liège in 1597

780–792. From murals, manuscripts, and metalwork

793–800. From architectural paintings at Versailles and a furniture marble inlay

801–809. From interior décor and illuminated choir books, France

810–817. From gilt and color-printed leatherwork

818–823. Painted tapestry designs by Robert de Cotte and others

824–835. French silk fabrics

836–852. Details from French tapestries and wall panels